*To:*

Mother Barbara
Mc Cray

*From:*

Myself

*Date:*

8-22-11 Birthday
8-26-11

© 2011 Summerside Press™
Minneapolis, MN 55438
www.summersidepress.com

Great Is Thy Faithfulness
A *Pocket Inspirations* Book

ISBN 978-1-60936-126-6

Excluding Scripture verses and divine pronouns, in some quotations references to men and masculine pronouns have been replaced with gender-neutral or feminine references.

Compiled by Barbara Farmer
Designed by Lisa and Jeff Franke

*Summerside Press is an inspirational publisher offering fresh, irresistible books to uplift the heart and engage the mind.*

Printed in USA.

# GREAT IS THY
## *Faithfulness*

summerside
PRESS

*All I have needed Thy hand hath provided;*
*Great is Thy faithfulness, Lord, unto me!*

THOMAS O. CHISHOLM

# Contents

*v*

# Introduction

God loves to show us, His children, that He is always faithful and He will never fail us. He takes delight when we completely depend on Him.

*Great Is Thy Faithfulness* is a collection of quotes and Bible verses specially selected to reassure you that God loves you with an everlasting love—that He knows every desire of your heart; that He will be faithful to every promise in His Word. Let these verses, quotations, and lyrics inspire you to put your faith in God's unfailing goodness.

Trust in the Lord, and may His great love encourage you always.

# Faithful Promises

Great faith isn't the ability to believe long
and far into the misty future. It's simply taking
God at His word and taking the next step.

JONI EARECKSON TADA

Now faith is being sure of what we hope for and
certain of what we do not see.... By faith we
understand that the universe was formed at God's
command, so that what is seen was not made
out of what was visible.... And without faith it
is impossible to please God, because anyone who
comes to him must believe that he exists and that
he rewards those who earnestly seek him.

HEBREWS 11:1, 3, 6 NIV

Faith is not passivity, but the passageway
to God's promises.

NEVA COYLE

God takes care of His own. He knows our
needs. He anticipates our crises. He is moved
by our weaknesses. He stands ready to come
to our rescue. And at just the right
moment He steps in and proves Himself
as our faithful heavenly Father.

CHARLES SWINDOLL

Faith goes up the stairs that love has made and
looks out the window which hope has opened.

CHARLES H. SPURGEON

*Let us draw near to God.... Let us hold
unswervingly to the hope we profess,
for he who promised is faithful.*

HEBREWS 10:22–23 NIV

# Guided by His Hand

To You, O LORD, I lift up my soul.
O my God, in You I trust....
Make me know Your ways,
O LORD; teach me Your paths.
Lead me in Your truth and teach me,
for You are the God of my salvation;
for You I wait all the day.
Remember, O LORD, Your compassion
and Your lovingkindnesses,
for they have been from of old.

PSALM 25:1–2, 4–6 NASB

We are of such value to God that He came to live
among us...and to guide us home. He will go
to any length to seek us, even to being lifted high
upon the cross to draw us back to Himself.
We can only respond by loving God for His love.

CATHERINE OF SIENNA

You guide me with your counsel,
leading me to a glorious destiny.

PSALM 73:24 NLT

Divine guidance is promised to us, and our faith must
therefore confidently look for and expect it.

HANNAH WHITALL SMITH

Pardon for sin and a peace that endureth
Thine own dear presence to cheer and to guide;
Strength for today and bright hope for tomorrow,
Blessings all mine, with ten thousand beside!

THOMAS O. CHISHOLM

The Lord is able to guide. The promises cover every
imaginable situation.... Take the hand He stretches out.

ELISABETH ELLIOT

*You guide me with your counsel,
leading me to a glorious destiny.*

PSALM 73:24 NLT

# Infinite Love

An infinite God can give all of Himself to each of His children. He does not distribute Himself that each may have a part, but to each one He gives all of Himself as fully as if there were no others.... His love has not changed. It hasn't cooled off, and it needs no increase because He has already loved us with infinite love and there is no way that infinitude can be increased.... He is the same yesterday, today, and forever!

A. W. TOZER

At the very heart and foundation of all God's dealings with us, however dark and mysterious they may be, we must dare to believe in and assert the infinite, unmerited, and unchanging love of God.

L. B. COWMAN

Christ did not die for people because they were intrinsically worth dying for, but because He is intrinsically love, and therefore loves infinitely.

C. S. LEWIS

Infinite and yet personal, personal and yet infinite,
God may be trusted because He is the True One.
He is true, He acts truly, and He speaks truly....
God's truthfulness is therefore foundational
for His trustworthiness.

OS GUINNESS

For the love of God is broader
Than the measure of man's mind
And the heart of the Eternal
Is most wonderfully kind.

FREDERICK W. FABER

*Take a long, hard look. See how great
he is—infinite, greater than anything you
could ever imagine or figure out!*

JOB 36:26 MSG

# The Grace of God

God, being rich in mercy, because of His great love with which He loved us, even when we were dead in our transgressions, made us alive together with Christ (by grace you have been saved), and raised us up with Him, and seated us with Him in the heavenly places in Christ Jesus, so that in the ages to come He might show the surpassing riches of His grace in kindness toward us in Christ Jesus. For by grace you have been saved through faith; and that not of yourselves, it is the gift of God; not as a result of works, so that no one may boast.

EPHESIANS 2:4–9 NASB

Grace means that God already loves us as much as an infinite God can possibly love.

PHILIP YANCEY

Tell of His wondrous faithfulness,
and sound His power abroad;
sing the sweet promise of His grace,
the love and truth of God.

ISAAC WATTS

Grace is something you can never get but can only
be given. There's no way to earn it or deserve it
or bring it about any more than you can deserve
the taste of raspberries and cream or earn good
looks.... A good night's sleep is grace and so are
good dreams. Most tears are grace. The smell of
rain is grace. Somebody loving you is grace.

FREDERICK BUECHNER

*God's grace is the oil that fills the lamp of love.*

HENRY WARD BEECHER

# Everything Is Possible

There will always be the unknown. There will always be the unprovable. But faith confronts those frontiers with a thrilling leap. Then life becomes vibrant with adventure!

Dr. Robert Schuller

Faith means you want God and want to want nothing else.... In faith there is movement and development. Each day something is new.

Brennan Manning

Faith is the first factor in a life devoted to service. Without faith, nothing is possible. With it, nothing is impossible.

Mary McLeod Bethune

Faith is not an effort, a striving, a ceaseless
seeking, as so many earnest souls suppose,
but rather a letting go, an abandonment,
an abiding rest in God that nothing,
not even the soul's shortcomings, can disturb.

As the beloved of God,
under the shadow of His wings—
and as the apple of God's eye—
the seeds of great faith live within us.

GARY SMALLEY AND JOHN TRENT

Faith is like a boomerang; begin using what you have
and it comes back to you in greater measure.

CHARLES L. ALLEN

*With men it is impossible, but not with God; for
with God all things are possible.*

MARK 10:27 NKJV

11

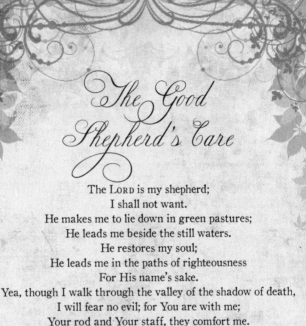

# The Good Shepherd's Care

The Lord is my shepherd;
I shall not want.
He makes me to lie down in green pastures;
He leads me beside the still waters.
He restores my soul;
He leads me in the paths of righteousness
For His name's sake.
Yea, though I walk through the valley of the shadow of death,
I will fear no evil; for You are with me;
Your rod and Your staff, they comfort me.
You prepare a table before me in the presence of my enemies;
You anoint my head with oil; my cup runs over.
Surely goodness and mercy shall follow me
All the days of my life;
And I will dwell in the house of the Lord
Forever.

Psalm 23:1–6 nkjv

When God has become our shepherd,
our refuge, our fortress, then we can reach out
to Him in the midst of a broken world and
feel at home while still on the way.

HENRI J. M. NOUWEN

The King of love my Shepherd is,
Whose goodness faileth never;
I nothing lack if I am His,
And He is mine forever.

SIR HENRY WILLIAMS BAKER

When at night you cannot sleep, talk to the
Shepherd and stop counting sheep.

⌘

*He tends his flock like a shepherd:
he gathers the lambs in his arms
and carries them close to his heart.*

ISAIAH 40:11 NIV

⌘

# God-Traveled Roads

How blessed all those in whom you live,
whose lives become roads you travel;
they wind through lonesome valleys, come upon brooks,
discover cool springs and pools brimming with rain!
God-traveled, these roads curve up the mountain,
and at the last turn—Zion! God in full view!

PSALM 84:5–7 MSG

I heard the voice of Jesus say:
"I am this dark world's light;
Look unto Me, thy morn shall rise,
And all thy day be bright."
I looked to Jesus, and I found
In Him my Star, my Sun:
And in that light of life I'll walk,
'Till traveling days are done!

HORATIUS BONAR

My child, listen to me and do as I say,
and you will have a long, good life.
I will teach you wisdom's ways
and lead you in straight paths.
When you walk, you won't be held back;
when you run, you won't stumble.
Take hold of my instructions; don't let them go.
Guard them, for they are the key to life.

PROVERBS 4:10–13 NLT

Two roads diverged in a wood, and I—
I took the one less traveled by,
And that has made all the difference.

ROBERT FROST

⟿⟾

*They travel lightly whom God's grace carries.*

THOMAS À KEMPIS

⟿⟾

# Joy and Strength

If one is joyful, it means that one is faithfully
living for God, and that nothing else counts; and
if one gives joy to others one is doing God's work.
With joy without and joy within, all is well.

JANET ERSKINE STUART

Sometimes in folk around me
With burdens, hurts and fears:
Through joyful, happy hours
And often through their tears:
In some loving act of kindness
As they show how much they care—
In the lives of folk around me
I find God reflected there.

CYRUS E. ALBERTSON

Live for today but hold your hands open
to tomorrow. Anticipate the future and its
changes with joy. There is a seed of God's love
in every event, every circumstance, every...
situation in which you may find yourself.

BARBARA JOHNSON

Finding acceptance with joy, whatever the
circumstances of life—whether they
are petty annoyances or fiery trials—
this is a living faith that grows.

MARY LOU STEIGLEDER

Life itself, every bit of health that we enjoy,
every hour of liberty and free enjoyment...
comes from the hand of God.

BILLY GRAHAM

*The joy of the LORD is your strength!*

NEHEMIAH 8:10 NLT

# The Majesty of God

O Lord, our Lord,
how majestic is your name in all the earth!
You have set your glory above the heavens....
When I consider your heavens,
the work of your fingers,
the moon and the stars,
which you have set in place,
what is man that you are mindful of him,
the son of man that you care for him?
You made him a little lower than the heavenly beings
and crowned him with glory and honor....
O Lord, our Lord,
how majestic is your name in all the earth!

PSALM 8:1, 3–5, 9 NIV

The God who holds the whole world in His hands
wraps Himself in the splendor of the sun's light
and walks among the clouds.

Forbid that I should walk through
Thy beautiful world with unseeing eyes:
Forbid that the lure of the market-place
should ever entirely steal my heart
away from the love of the
open acres and the green trees:
Forbid that under the low roof of
workshop or office or study I should ever
forget Thy great overarching sky.

John Baillie

Those who see God will partake of life,
for the splendor of God is life-giving.

Irenaeus

*Savor little glimpses of
God's goodness and His majesty,
thankful for the gift of them.*

# Our Divine Imprint

The God of the universe—the One who created
everything and holds it all in His hand—
created each of us in His image, to bear His
likeness, His imprint. It is only when Christ dwells
within our hearts, radiating the pure light of His
love through our humanity, that we discover who
we are and what we were intended to be.

WENDY MOORE

In the very beginning it was God who formed us
by His Word. He made us in His own image. God
was spirit and He gave us a spirit so that He could
come into us and mingle His own life with our life.

MADAME JEANNE GUYON

You are a little less than angels, crown of creation,
image of God. Each person is a revelation,
a transfiguration, a waiting for Him to manifest Himself.

EDWARD FARRELL

Made in His image, we can have real meaning,
and we can have real knowledge through
what He has communicated to us.

FRANCIS SCHAEFFER

Human love would never have the power it has
were it not rooted in an express image of God.

J. MOUROUX

For in Him all the fullness of Deity dwells in bodily form,
and in Him you have been made complete.

COLOSSIANS 2:9–10 NASB

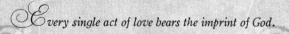

*Every single act of love bears the imprint of God.*

# God With Us

God gets down on His knees among us; gets on our level and shares Himself with us. He does not reside afar off and send diplomatic messages, He kneels among us…. God shares Himself generously and graciously.

EUGENE PETERSON

God loves to look at us, and loves it when we will look back at Him. Even when we try to run away from our troubles…God will find us, bless us, even when we feel most alone, unsure…. God will find a way to let us know that He is with us *in this place*, wherever we are.

KATHLEEN NORRIS

When all is said and done, the last word is Immanuel—God-With-Us.

ISAIAH 8:10 MSG

God is there with us even in the darkest hours,
and we can never escape His encompassing love.

DR. JAMES DOBSON

God is changeless. He will be unusual. He won't
strike an average anywhere. He will get out
of bounds and meet us on any level with His
patience and His love and His bounty.

JEAN CHURCH

You are in the Beloved...therefore infinitely dear
to the Father, unspeakably precious to Him.
You are never, not for one second, alone.

NORMAN DOWTY

*My Presence will go with you,
and I will give you rest.*

EXODUS 33:14 NIV

# Mighty to Keep

God, who is our dwelling place, is also our fortress.
It can only mean one thing, and that is, that if
we will but live in our dwelling place, we shall be
perfectly safe and secure from every assault.

Hannah Whitall Smith

God is adequate as our keeper.... Your faith will not
fail while God sustains it; you are not strong enough
to fall away while God is resolved to hold you.

J. I. Packer

He who dwells in the shelter of the Most High
will abide in the shadow of the Almighty.
I will say to the Lord, "My refuge and my fortress,
my God, in whom I trust!"

Psalm 91:1–2 nasb

May the God of love and peace set your
heart at rest and speed you on your journey.
May He meanwhile shelter you from disturbance
by others in the place of complete plenitude
where you will repose for ever in the
vision of peace, in the security of trust,
and in the restful enjoyment of His riches.

RAYMOND OF PENYAFORT

Let my soul take refuge...beneath the shadow
of Your wings: let my heart, this sea of restless waves,
find peace in You, O God.

AUGUSTINE

*God stands fast as your rock,*
*steadfast as your safeguard,*
*sleepless as your watcher,*
*valiant as your champion.*

CHARLES H. SPURGEON

# Renewed by His Beauty

The joyful birds prolong the strain,
their song with every spring renewed;
the air we breathe, and falling rain,
each softly whispers: God is good.

JOHN HAMPDEN GURNEY

All the world is an utterance of the Almighty.
Its countless beauties, its exquisite adaptations,
all speak to you of Him.

PHILLIPS BROOKS

Be still, and in the quiet moments, listen to the voice of
your heavenly Father. His words can renew your spirit...
no one knows you and your needs like He does.

JANET L. SMITH

Lord...give me the gift of faith to be renewed and
shared with others each day. Teach me to live
this moment only, looking neither to the past
with regret, nor the future with apprehension.
Let love be my aim and my life a prayer.

ROSEANN ALEXANDER-ISHAM

Our Creator would never have made such
lovely days, and given us the deep hearts
to enjoy them, above and beyond all thought,
unless we were meant to be immortal.

NATHANIEL HAWTHORNE

In the morning let our hearts gaze upon God's love
and the love He has allowed us to share, and in the
beauty of that vision, let us go forth to meet the day.

ROY LESSIN

*Worship the LORD in the beauty of holiness!*

PSALM 96:9 NKJV

# Walking with God

My Lord God, I have no idea where I am going.
I do not see the road ahead of me. I cannot
know for certain where it will end.... But I
believe that the desire to please You does in fact
please You. And I hope I have that desire in
all that I am doing. I hope that I will never do
anything apart from that desire. And I know
that if I do this, You will lead me by the right
road though I may know nothing about it.

Therefore will I trust You always though I may
seem to be lost and in the shadow of death. I
will not fear, for You are ever with me. And
You will never leave me to face my perils alone.

THOMAS MERTON

Faith is meant to be lived moment by moment.
It isn't some broad, general outline—it's a long
walk with a real Person.

JONI EARECKSON TADA

Joy is more than my spontaneous expression
of laughter, gaiety, and lightness. It is deeper than
an emotional expression of happiness. Joy is
a growing, evolving manifestation of God
in my life as I walk with Him.

Bonnie Monson

I would rather walk with God in the dark
than go alone in the light.

Mary Gardiner Brainard

We don't walk spiritually by electric light,
but by a hand-held lantern. And a lantern shows
only the next step—not several steps ahead.

Amy Carmichael

*Yet I am always with you;
you hold me by my right hand.*

Psalm 73:23 niv

# God's Eternal Love

The LORD is like a father to his children,
tender and compassionate to those who fear him.
For he knows how weak we are;
he remembers we are only dust.
Our days on earth are like grass;
like wildflowers, we bloom and die.
The wind blows, and we are gone—
as though we had never been here.
But the love of the LORD remains forever....
The LORD has made the heavens his throne;
from there he rules over everything.

PSALM 103:13–17, 19 NLT

Amid the ebb and flow of the passing world,
our God remains unmoved,
and His throne endures forever.

ROBERT COLEMAN

The reason we can dare to risk loving others is
that "God has for Christ's sake loved us."
Think of it! We are loved eternally,
totally, individually, unreservedly!
Nothing can take God's love away.

GLORIA GAITHER

The impetus of God's love comes from within
Himself, to share with us His life and love. It is a
beautiful, eternal gift, held out to us in the hands
of love. All we have to do is say "Yes!"

JOHN POWELL, S.J.

*Great is his love toward us,
and the faithfulness of the LORD
endures forever.*

PSALM 117:2 NIV

# Encountering God

God is with us in the midst of our daily,
routine lives. In the middle of cleaning
the house or driving somewhere in the
pickup.... Often it's in the middle of the
most mundane task that He lets us know He
is there with us. We realize, then, that there
can be no "ordinary" moments for people
who live their lives with Jesus.

MICHAEL CARD

Much of what is sacred is hidden in the
ordinary, everyday moments of our lives.
To see something of the sacred in those
moments takes slowing down so we can live
our lives more reflectively.

KEN GIRE

When a job is offered to God in faith, He blesses
it and it becomes a means not only of serving
Him in this world, but of encountering Him here.

BEN PATTERSON

We encounter God in the ordinariness
of life, not in the search for spiritual highs
and extraordinary, mystical experiences,
but in our simple presence in life.

BRENNAN MANNING

If each moment is sacred—a time and place
where we encounter God—life itself is sacred.

JEAN M. BLOMQUIST

*This is how we experience his deep and
abiding presence in us: by the Spirit he gave us.*

1 JOHN 3:24 MSG

8-26-11

# Always There

We need never shout across the spaces to an
absent God. He is nearer than our own soul,
closer than our most secret thoughts.

A. W. Tozer

God is always present in the temple of your
heart...His home. And when you come in to meet
Him there, you find that it is the one place of deep
satisfaction where every longing is met.

Always be in a state of expectancy, and see that
you leave room for God to come in as He likes.

Oswald Chambers

Nothing we can do will make the Father love us less;
nothing we do can make Him love us more.
He loves us unconditionally with an everlasting love.

NANCIE CARMICHAEL

How could I be anything but quite happy
if I believed always that all the past is forgiven,
and all the present furnished with power,
and all the future bright with hope.

JAMES SMETHAM

God's love...is ever and always, eternally
present to all who fear him, making
everything right for them and their children
as they follow his Covenant ways.

PSALM 103:17–18 MSG

*We are ever so secure in the everlasting arms.*

# Faithful in Prayer

Prayer is such an ordinary, everyday, mundane thing.
Certainly, people who pray are no more saints than the
rest of us. Rather, they are people who want to share a
life with God, to love and be loved, to speak and to listen,
to work and to be at rest in the presence of God.

ROBERTA BONDI

So faith bounds forward to its goal in God,
and love can trust her Lord to lead her there;
upheld by Him my soul is following hard,
till God hath full fulfilled my deepest prayer.

FREDERICK BROOK

Nothing in your daily life is so insignificant
and so inconsequential that God will not help
you by answering your prayer.

OLE HALLESBY

Can we find a friend so faithful,
Who will all our sorrows share?
Jesus knows our every weakness:
Take it to the Lord in prayer.

GEORGE SCRIVEN

Faith is the bucket of power lowered by the rope of prayer into the well of God's abundance. What we bring up depends upon what we let down. We have every encouragement to use a big bucket.

VIRGINIA WHITMAN

I know that God is faithful. I know that He answers prayers, many times in ways I may not understand.

SHEILA WALSH

*Give your burdens to the Lord,
and he will take care of you.*

PSALM 55:22 NLT

# God Is Passing By

Friendships, family ties, the companionship of little children, an autumn forest flung in prodigality against a deep blue sky, the intricate design and haunting fragrance of a flower, the counterpoint of a Bach fugue or the melodic line of a Beethoven sonata, the fluted note of bird song, the glowing glory of a sunset: the world is aflame with things of eternal moment.

E. MARGARET CLARKSON

The awe that we sense or ought to sense when standing in the presence of a human being is a moment of intuition for the likeness of God which is concealed in His essence.

ABRAHAM JOSHUA HESCHEL

If we take Jesus at His word, all of us are contemplatives in the heart of the world, for if we have faith, we are continually in His presence.

MOTHER TERESA

The day is done,
The sun has set,
Yet light still tints the sky;
My heart stands still
In reverence,
For God is passing by.

RUTH ALLA WAGER

We are always in the presence of God.... There is never a nonsacred moment! His presence never diminishes. Our awareness of His presence may falter, but the reality of His presence never changes.

MAX LUCADO

*Where morning dawns and evening fades you call forth songs of joy.*

PSALM 65:8 NIV

# Boundless Life

I ask—ask the God of our Master, Jesus
Christ, the God of glory—to make you
intelligent and discerning in knowing him
personally, your eyes focused and clear, so
that you can see exactly what it is he is calling
you to do, grasp the immensity of this glorious
way of life he has for his followers, oh, the
utter extravagance of his work in us who trust
him—endless energy, boundless strength!

EPHESIANS 1:17–19 MSG

The Creator of all thinks enough of you
to have sent Someone very special so that
you might have life—abundantly, joyfully,
completely, and victoriously.

I have known art and beauty, music
and gladness; I have known friendship and
love and family ties; but it is certain
that till we see God in the world—
God in the bright and boundless universe—
we never know the highest joy.

ORVILLE DEWEY

How Sweet the name of Jesus...
the rock on which I build,
my shield and hiding place,
my never failing treasury,
filled with boundless stores of grace.

JOHN NEWTON

*The resource from which [God] gives is
boundless, measureless, unlimited, unending,
abundant, almighty, and eternal.*

JACK HAYFORD

# Trustworthy Guide

I'll take the hand of those who don't know the
way, who can't see where they're going. I'll
be a personal guide to them, directing them
through unknown country. I'll be right there
to show them what roads to take, make sure
they don't fall into the ditch. These are the
things I'll be doing for them—sticking with
them, not leaving them for a minute.

ISAIAH 42:16 MSG

Heaven often seems distant and unknown,
but if He who made the road...is our guide,
we need not fear to lose the way.

HENRY VAN DYKE

Whether you turn to the right or to the left,
your ears will hear a voice behind you, saying,
"This is the way; walk in it."

ISAIAH 30:21 NIV

Keep close to your rule, the Word of God,
and to your guide, the Spirit of God,
and never be afraid of expecting too much.

JOHN WESLEY

The LORD says, "I will guide you along
the best pathway for your life.
I will advise you and watch over you."

PSALM 32:8 NLT

∽⊰⊱∾

*God shall be my hope, my stay,
my guide and lantern to my feet.*

WILLIAM SHAKESPEARE

∽⊰⊱∾

# Blessing on Blessing

Bless the LORD, O my soul;
And all that is within me, bless His holy name!
Bless the LORD, O my soul,
And forget not all His benefits:
Who forgives all your iniquities,
Who heals all your diseases,
Who redeems your life from destruction,
Who crowns you with lovingkindness
and tender mercies,
Who satisfies your mouth with good things,
So that your youth is renewed like the eagle's.

PSALM 103:1–5 NKJV

God is a rich and bountiful Father, and He does not
forget His children, nor withhold from them anything
which it would be to their advantage to receive.

J. K. MACLEAN

His overflowing love delights to make us
partakers of the bounties He graciously imparts.

HANNAH MORE

Christ is no Moses, no exactor,
no giver of laws, but a giver of grace,
a Savior; he is infinite mercy and goodness,
freely and bountifully given to us.

MARTIN LUTHER

I will send down showers in season;
there will be showers of blessing.

EZEKIEL 34:26 NIV

God, who is love—who is, if I may say
it this way, made out of love—simply cannot
help but shed blessing on blessing upon us.

HANNAH WHITALL SMITH

We benefit eternally by God's
being just what He is.

45

# God Waits for Us

God has put into each of our lives a void that
cannot be filled by the world. We may leave God or
put Him on hold, but He is always there, patiently
waiting for us...to turn back to Him.

EMILIE BARNES

With God, one day is as good as a thousand
years, a thousand years as a day. God isn't late
with his promise as some measure lateness. He is
restraining himself on account of you, holding back
the End because he doesn't want anyone lost.
He's giving everyone space and time to change.

2 PETER 3:8–9 MSG

Lift up your eyes. Your heavenly Father
waits to bless you—in inconceivable ways to make
your life what you never dreamed it could be.

ANNE ORTLUND

God is waiting for us to come to Him with our needs....
God's throne room is always open.

CHARLES STANLEY

The God who hears is also the one who speaks. He has
spoken and is still speaking. Humanity remains His
project, not its own, and His initiatives are always at
work among us. He certainly "gives us space," as we say,
and this is essential. But He continues to speak in ways
that serious inquirers can hear if they will.

DALLAS WILLARD

*God waits for us in the inner sanctuary
of the soul. He welcomes us there.*

RICHARD J. FOSTER

# *Nothing but Grace*

When we focus on God, the scene changes. He's in control of our lives; nothing lies outside the realm of His redemptive grace. Even when we make mistakes, fail in relationships, or deliberately make bad choices, God can redeem us.

PENELOPE J. STOKES

There is nothing but God's grace. We walk upon it; we breathe it; we live and die by it; it makes the nails and axles of the universe.

ROBERT LOUIS STEVENSON

Grace is no stationary thing, it is ever becoming. It is flowing straight out of God's heart. Grace does nothing but re-form and convey God. Grace makes the soul conformable to the will of God. God, the ground of the soul, and grace go together.

MEISTER ECKHART

Grace and gratitude belong together
like heaven and earth.
Grace evokes gratitude like the
voice an echo. Gratitude follows grace
as thunder follows lightning.

KARL BARTH

Grace is the dynamic outpouring of God's loving
nature that flows into and through creation in an
endless self-offering of healing, love, illumination,
and reconciliation. It is a gift that we are free
to ignore, reject, ask for, or simply accept.

DR. GERALD G. MAY

*The LORD is compassionate and gracious,
slow to anger, abounding in love.*

PSALM 103:8 NIV

# New Light

Into all our lives, in many simple, familiar, homely ways, God infuses this element of joy from the surprises of life, which unexpectedly brighten our days, and fill our eyes with light.

SAMUEL LONGFELLOW

Lord, let the glow of Your love
Through my whole being shine;
Fill me with gladness from above
And hold me by strength divine.
Lord, make Your light in my heart
Glow radiant and clear, never to part.

MARGARET FISHBACK POWERS

Brightness of my Father's glory,
Sunshine of my Father's face,
Let thy glory e'er shine on me,
Fill me with Thy grace.

JEAN SOPHIA PIGOTT

It doesn't take a huge spotlight to draw attention
to how great our God is. All it takes is for one
committed person to so let his light shine before men,
that a world lost in darkness welcomes the light.

GARY SMALLEY AND JOHN TRENT

Whoso draws nigh to God
One step through doubtings dim,
God will advance a mile
In blazing light to him.

Every good and perfect gift is from above,
coming down from the Father of the heavenly lights,
who does not change like shifting shadows.

JAMES 1:17 NIV

*God's touch...lights the world with*
*color and renews our hearts with life.*

JANET L. SMITH

# The Living Word

Every part of Scripture is God-breathed
and useful one way or another—showing us truth,
exposing our rebellion, correcting our mistakes,
training us to live God's way. Through the Word
we are put together and shaped up
for the tasks God has for us.

2 TIMOTHY 3:16–17 MSG

Amid ancient lore the Word of God stands unique
and pre-eminent. Wonderful in its construction,
admirable in its adaptation, it contains truths
that a child may comprehend, and mysteries
into which angels desire to look.

FRANCES ELLEN WATKINS HARPER

The God who created the vast resources of the universe is also the inventor of the human mind. His inspired words of encouragement guarantee us that we can live above our circumstances.

Dr. James Dobson

For the word of God is living and active and sharper than any two-edged sword...able to judge the thoughts and intentions of the heart.

Hebrews 4:12–13 nasb

When we give the Word of God space to live in our heart, the Spirit of God will use it to take root, penetrating the earthiest recesses of our lives.

Ken Gire

❧

*The Word of God, Jesus Christ, on account of His great love for mankind, became what we are in order to make us what He is Himself.*

Irenaeus

❧

# God Is Good

All that is good, all that is true, all that is beautiful,
all that is beneficent, be it great or small, be it perfect
or fragmentary, natural as well as supernatural,
moral as well as material, comes from God.

JOHN HENRY NEWMAN

God never abandons anyone on whom He has set
His love; nor does Christ, the good shepherd, ever lose
track of His sheep. How slow we are to believe
in God as God, sovereign, all-seeing, and almighty!
We need to "wait upon the Lord" in meditations
on His majesty, till we find our strength renewed
through the writing of these things upon our hearts.

J. I. PACKER

Open your mouth and taste, open your eyes
and see—how good God is. Blessed are you who
run to him. Worship God if you want the best;
worship opens doors to all his goodness.

PSALM 34:8–9 MSG

We walk without fear, full of hope and courage
and strength to do His will, waiting for the
endless good which He is always giving as fast
as He can get us able to take it in.

GEORGE MACDONALD

*I am still confident in this:*
*I will see the goodness of the LORD*
*in the land of the living.*

PSALM 27:13 NIV

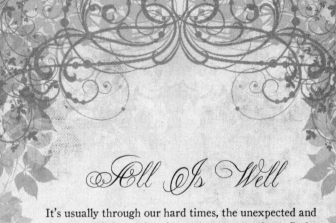

# All Is Well

It's usually through our hard times, the unexpected and not-according-to-plan times, that we experience God in more intimate ways. We discover an unquenchable longing to know Him more. It's a passion that isn't concerned that life fall within certain predictable lines, but a passion that pursues God and knows He is relentless in His pursuit of each one of us.

WENDY MOORE

A living, loving God can and does make His presence felt, can and does speak to us in the silence of our hearts, can and does warm and caress us till we no longer doubt that He is near, that He is here.

BRENNAN MANNING

In difficulties, I can drink freely of God's power
and experience His touch of refreshment and blessing—
much like an invigorating early spring rain.

ANABEL GILLHAM

Life from the Center is a life of unhurried peace and
power. It is simple. It is serene.... We need not get
frantic. He is at the helm. And when our little day
is done, we lie down quietly in peace, for all is well.

THOMAS R. KELLY

Lord, you have been our dwelling place throughout
all generations. Before the mountains were born
or you brought forth the earth and the world,
from everlasting to everlasting you are God.

PSALM 90:1–2 NIV

*Before me, even as behind,*
*God is, and all is well.*

JOHN GREENLEAF WHITTIER

# God Knows

The simple fact of being...in the presence of
the Lord and of showing Him all that I think,
feel, sense, and experience, without trying to
hide anything, must please Him. Somehow,
somewhere, I know that He loves me, even though
I do not feel that love as I can feel a human
embrace, even though I do not hear a voice as I
hear human words of consolation.... God is greater
than my senses, greater than my thoughts, greater
than my heart. I do believe that He touches me in
places that are unknown even to myself.

HENRI J. M. NOUWEN

Pour out your heart to God your Father.
He understands you better than you do.

God possesses infinite knowledge and an awareness which is uniquely His. At all times, even in the midst of any type of suffering, I can realize that He knows, loves, watches, understands, and more than that, He has a purpose.

BILLY GRAHAM

Living a life of faith means never knowing where you are being led. But it does mean loving and knowing the One who is leading.

OSWALD CHAMBERS

Faith is not believing that God can— it's knowing that He will.

*If anyone loves God, he is known by Him.*

1 CORINTHIANS 8:3 NASB

# New Every Morning

With God, life is eternal—both in quality and length.
There is no joy comparable to the joy of discovering
something new from God, about God. If the continuing
life is a life of joy, we will go on discovering, learning.

EUGENIA PRICE

This I recall to my mind,
Therefore I have hope.
The LORD's lovingkindnesses indeed never cease,
For His compassions never fail.
They are new every morning;
Great is Your faithfulness.
"The LORD is my portion," says my soul,
"Therefore I have hope in Him."

LAMENTATIONS 3:21–24 NASB

That is God's call to us—simply to be people who are content to live close to Him and to renew the kind of life in which the closeness is felt and experienced.

THOMAS MERTON

A quiet morning with a loving God puts the events of the upcoming day into proper perspective.

JANETTE OKE

Today is unique! It has never occurred before, and it will never be repeated. At midnight it will end, quietly, suddenly, totally. Forever. But the hours between now and then are opportunities with eternal possibilities.

CHARLES R. SWINDOLL

*Satisfy us in the morning with your unfailing love, that we may sing for joy and be glad all our days.*

PSALM 90:14 NIV

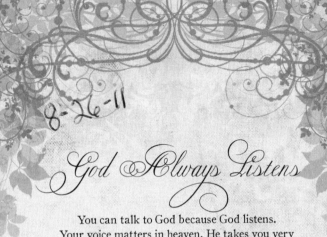

8-26-11

# God Always Listens

You can talk to God because God listens.
Your voice matters in heaven. He takes you very
seriously. When you enter His presence, the
attendants turn to you to hear your voice.
No need to fear that you will be ignored. Even if you
stammer or stumble, even if what you have to say
impresses no one, it impresses God—and He listens.

MAX LUCADO

Open wide the windows of our spirits and fill
us full of light; open wide the door of our hearts,
that we may receive and entertain Thee with
all our powers of adoration.

CHRISTINA ROSSETTI

*8-26-11*

*Lord please listen to my Cry for Tammy, please*

We come this morning—
Like empty pitchers to a full fountain,
With no merits of our own,
O Lord—open up a window of heaven...
And listen this morning.

JAMES WELDON JOHNSON

I love the Lord because he hears my prayers
and answers them.
Because he bends down and listens,
I will pray as long as I breathe!

PSALM 116:1–2 TLB

God listens in compassion and love, just like we do when
our children come to us. He delights in our presence.

RICHARD J. FOSTER

When we call on God, He bends down His ear to
listen, as a father bends down to listen to his little child.

ELIZABETH CHARLES

# Comfort Sweet

All God's glory and beauty come from within,
and there He delights to dwell. His visits there are
frequent, His conversation sweet, His comforts
refreshing, His peace passing all understanding.

THOMAS À KEMPIS

Every now and again take a good look at
something not made with hands—a mountain, a
star, the turn of a stream. There will come to you
wisdom and patience and solace and, above all, the
assurance that you are not alone in the world.

SIDNEY LOVETT

God comforts. He lays His right hand
on the wounded soul...and He says, as if that one
were the only soul in all the universe:
O greatly beloved, fear not: peace be unto thee.

AMY CARMICHAEL

There is a place of comfort sweet
Near to the heart of God,
A place where we our Savior meet,
Near to the heart of God....
Hold us who wait before Thee
Near to the heart of God.

CLELAND B. MCAFEE

Now may our Lord Jesus Christ Himself and God our
Father, who has loved us and given us eternal comfort
and good hope by grace, comfort and strengthen
your hearts in every good work and word.

2 THESSALONIANS 2:16–17 NASB

*God comforts. He doesn't pity. He picks us up,
dries our tears, soothes our fears,
and lifts our thoughts beyond the hurt.*

DR. ROBERT SCHULLER

# Seek the Lord

The God who made the world and everything in it is
the Lord of heaven and earth.... He himself gives all men
life and breath and everything else.... God did this so
that men would seek him and perhaps reach out for him
and find him, though he is not far from each one of us.
"For in him we live, and move, and have our being."

ACTS 17:24–28 NIV

If you are seeking after God,
you may be sure of this:
God is seeking you much more.
He is the Lover, and you are His beloved.
He has promised Himself to you.

JOHN OF THE CROSS

The ability to see and the practice of seeing God
and God's world comes through a process of
seeking and growing in intimacy with Him.

DALLAS WILLARD

God is not an elusive dream or a phantom to
chase, but a divine person to know. He does not
avoid us, but seeks us. When we seek Him, the
contact is instantaneous.

NEVA COYLE

Prayer enlarges the heart until it is capable of
containing God's gift of Himself. Ask and seek,
and your heart will grow big enough to receive
Him and keep Him as your own.

MOTHER TERESA

*love those who love me; and those who
diligently seek me will find me.*

PROVERBS 8:17 NASB

# God's Thoughts

Your thoughts—how rare, how beautiful!
God, I'll never comprehend them!
I couldn't even begin to count them—
any more than I could count the sand of the sea.
Oh, let me rise in the morning and live always with you!

PSALM 139:17–18 MSG

Have you ever thought that in every action
of grace in your heart you have the whole
omnipotence of God engaged to bless you?

ANDREW MURRAY

God has designs on our future...and He has designed
us for the future. He has given us something
to do in the future that no one else can do.

RUTH SENTER

"My thoughts are nothing like your thoughts,"
says the LORD.
"And my ways are far beyond anything
you could imagine.
For just as the heavens are higher than the earth,
so my ways are higher than your ways
and my thoughts higher than your thoughts."

ISAIAH 55:8–9 NLT

The soul is a temple, and God is silently building
it by night and by day. Precious thoughts
are building it; unselfish love is building it;
all-penetrating faith is building it.

HENRY WARD BEECHER

⁓⋙⋘⁓

*Night by night I will lie down
and sleep in the thought of God.*

WILLIAM MOUNTFORD

⁓⋙⋘⁓

# Every Need

God wants nothing from us except our needs,
and these furnish Him with room to display His bounty
when He supplies them freely.... Not what I have,
but what I do not have, is the first point of contact
between my soul and God.

CHARLES H. SPURGEON

Jesus Christ has brought every need, every joy,
every gratitude, every hope of ours before God. He
accompanies us and brings us into the presence of God.

DIETRICH BONHOEFFER

Just as there comes a warm sunbeam into every cottage
window, so comes a love—born of God's care
for every separate need.

NATHANIEL HAWTHORNE

Each of us may be sure that if God sends us on stony
paths He will provide us with strong shoes,
and He will not send us out on any journey
for which He does not equip us well.

ALEXANDER MACLAREN

The "air" which our souls need also envelops all of us
at all times and on all sides. God is round about us...on
every hand, with many-sided and all-sufficient grace.

OLE HALLESBY

Faith allows us to continually delight in life since
we have placed our needs in God's hands.

JANET L. SMITH

*My God is changeless in his love for me,
and he will come and help me.*

PSALM 59:10 TLB

# God Is Always Here

God is here! I hear His voice
While thrushes make the woods rejoice.
I touch His robe each time I place
My hand against a pansy's face.
I breathe His breath if I but pass
Verbenas trailing through the grass.
God is here! From every tree
His leafy fingers beckon me.

MADELEINE AARON

The beauty of the earth, the beauty of the sky,
the order of the stars, the sun, the moon...their very
loveliness is their confession of God: for who
made these lovely mutable things, but He who
is Himself unchangeable beauty?

AUGUSTINE

If there is a God who speaks anywhere, surely
He speaks here: through waking up and working,
through going away and coming back again,
through people you read and books you meet,
through falling asleep in the dark.

FREDERICK BUECHNER

God wants us to approach life full of expectancy
that God is going to be at work in every situation
as we release our faith in Him.

COLIN URQUHART

I love to think of nature as an unlimited
broadcasting station through which God speaks
to us every hour, if only we will tune in.

GEORGE WASHINGTON CARVER

*Let the glory of the LORD endure forever;
let the LORD be glad in His works.*

PSALM 104:31 NASB

# Free to Live

GOD, your God, will cut away the thick calluses
on your heart and your children's hearts,
freeing you to love GOD, your God, with your
whole heart and soul and live, really live....
And you will make a new start, listening obediently
to GOD, keeping all his commandments that
I'm commanding you today. GOD, your God,
will outdo himself in making things go well for you....
Love GOD, your God. Walk in his ways.
Keep his commandments, regulations, and rules
so that you will live, really live, live exuberantly,
blessed by GOD.... Love GOD, your God, listening
obediently to him, firmly embracing him.
Oh yes, he is life itself.

DEUTERONOMY 30:6–9, 16, 20 MSG

We are forgiven and righteous because of Christ's sacrifice; therefore we are pleasing to God in spite of our failures. Christ alone is the source of our forgiveness, freedom, joy, and purpose.

ROBERT S. McGEE

In almost everything that touches our everyday life on earth, God is pleased when we're pleased. He wills that we be as free as birds to soar and sing our maker's praise without anxiety.

A. W. TOZER

By Jesus' gracious, kindly Spirit, He moves in our lives, sharing His very own life with us.... He introduces the exotic fruits of His own person into the prepared soil of our hearts; there they take root and flourish.

W. PHILLIP KELLER

*I asked God for all things that I might enjoy life.*
*He gave me life that I might enjoy all things.*

# Always a Way

Perhaps this moment is unclear, but let it be—
even if the next, and many moments after that are
unclear, let them be. Trust that God will help you
work them out, and that all the unclear moments
will bring you to that moment of clarity and action
when you are known by Him and know Him. These
are the better and brighter moments of His blessing.

WENDY MOORE

The temptations in your life are no different
from what others experience. And God is faithful.
He will not allow the temptation to be more than
you can stand. When you are tempted, he will
show you a way out so that you can endure.

1 CORINTHIANS 10:13 NLT

He writes in characters too grand
for our short sight to understand.
We catch but broken strokes
and try to fathom all the withered hopes
Of death, of life,
the endless war, the useless strife....
But there, with larger, clearer sight,
we shall see this: His way was right.

JOHN OXENHAM

When we pray we should keep in mind all of the
shortcomings and excesses we feel, and pour them out
freely to God, our faithful Father, who is ready to help.

MARTIN LUTHER

*You are my help and my deliverer.*

PSALM 40:17 NIV

# You Matter to Him

The God who created, names, and numbers
the stars in the heavens also numbers the
hairs of my head.... He pays attention
to very big things and to very small ones.
What matters to me matters to Him,
and that changes my life.

ELISABETH ELLIOT

What matters supremely is not the fact that I know
God, but the larger fact which underlies it—
the fact that He knows me. I am graven on the
palms of His hands. I am never out of His mind.
All my knowledge of Him depends on His sustained
initiative in knowing me. I know Him because He
first knew me, and continues to know me.

J. I. PACKER

One hundred years from today
your present income will be inconsequential.
One hundred years from now
it won't matter if you got that big break....
It will greatly matter that you knew God.

DAVID SHIBLEY

I'm not saying that I have this all together,
that I have it made. But I am well on my way,
reaching out for Christ, who has
so wondrously reached out for me.

PHILIPPIANS 3:12 MSG

*Something deep in all of us yearns
for God's beauty, and we can find it
no matter where we are.*

SUE MONK KIDD

# Faithful to All Generations

Life is no brief candle to me. It is a...splendid torch...
and I want to make it burn as brightly as possible
before handing it over to future generations.

GEORGE BERNARD SHAW

Know therefore that the LORD your God is God;
he is the faithful God, keeping his covenant
of love to a thousand generations of those
who love him and keep his commands.

DEUTERONOMY 7:9 NIV

Creating a family in this turbulent world is an act
of faith, a wager that against all odds there will
be a future, that love can last, that the heart
can triumph against all adversities and even
against the grinding wheel of time.

DEAN KOONTZ

Enter his gates with thanksgiving
and his courts with praise;
give thanks to him and praise his name.
For the LORD is good and his love endures forever;
his faithfulness continues through all generations.

PSALM 100:4–5 NIV

There is nothing quite so deeply satisfying as the
solidarity of a family united across the generations
and miles by a common faith and history.

SARA WENGER SHENK

I will sing of the mercies of the LORD forever;
With my mouth will I make known
Your faithfulness to all generations.

PSALM 89:1 NKJV

*In following our everlasting God,
we touch the things that last forever.*

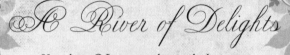

# A River of Delights

Your love, O LORD, reaches to the heavens,
your faithfulness to the skies.
Your righteousness is like the mighty mountains,
your justice like the great deep....
How priceless is your unfailing love!
Both high and low among men
find refuge in the shadow of your wings.
They feast on the abundance of your house;
you give them drink from your river of delights.
For with you is the fountain of life;
in your light we see light.

PSALM 36:5–9 NIV

From God, great and small, rich and poor, draw living
water from a living spring, and those who serve Him
freely and gladly will receive grace answering to grace.

THOMAS À KEMPIS

Like supernatural effervescence, praise will sometimes
bubble up from the joy of simply knowing Christ.
Praise like that is...delight. Pure pleasure!

JONI EARECKSON TADA

God's love is like a river springing up in the Divine
Substance and flowing endlessly through His creation,
filling all things with life and goodness and strength.

THOMAS MERTON

Those who drink the water I give will never
be thirsty again. It becomes a fresh, bubbling
spring within them, giving them eternal life.

JOHN 4:14 NLT

*Loving Creator, help me reawaken my childlike
sense of wonder at the delights of Your world!*

MARILYN MORGAN HELLEBERG

# Rest in Him

My soul finds rest in God alone;
my salvation comes from him.
He alone is my rock and my salvation;
he is my fortress, I will never be shaken....
My salvation and my honor depend on God;
he is my mighty rock, my refuge.
Trust in him at all times, O people;
pour out your hearts to him,
for God is our refuge.

PSALM 62:1–2, 7–8 NIV

Joy comes from knowing God loves me and
knows who I am and where I'm going...that my
future is secure as I rest in Him.

DR. JAMES DOBSON

God provides resting places as well as
working places. Rest, then, and be thankful when
He brings you, wearied, to a wayside well.

L. B. Cowman

If God gives such attention to the appearance of
wildflowers—most of which are never even seen—
don't you think he'll attend to you, take pride
in you, do his best for you?... Steep your life in
God-reality, God-initiative, God-provisions.
Don't worry about missing out. You'll find all
your everyday human concerns will be met.

Matthew 6:30, 33 msg

When God finds a soul that rests in Him
and is not easily moved...to this same soul
He gives the joy of His presence.

Catherine of Genoa

*Rest in the Lord, and wait patiently for Him.*

Psalm 37:7 nkjv

# God at Work in Us

To pray is to change. This is a great grace.
How good of God to provide a path whereby
our lives can be taken over by love and joy and peace
and patience and kindness and goodness
and faithfulness and gentleness and self-control.

RICHARD J. FOSTER

The wonder of our Lord is that He is so accessible
to us in the common things of our lives: the cup
of water...breaking of the bread...welcoming
children into our arms...fellowship over a meal...
giving thanks. A simple attitude of caring,
listening, and lovingly telling the truth.

NANCIE CARMICHAEL

For God is, indeed, a wonderful Father
who longs to pour out His mercy upon us,
and whose majesty is so great that
He can transform us from deep within.

TERESA OF AVILA

If God is here for us and not elsewhere, then in
fact *this place* is holy and *this moment* is sacred.

ISABEL ANDERS

Our joy will be complete if we remain
in His love—for His love is personal, intimate,
real, living, delicate, faithful love.

MOTHER TERESA

*Create in me a clean heart, O God,*
*And renew a steadfast spirit within me.*

PSALM 51:10 NKJV

# Footpath to Peace

To be glad of life, because it gives you the chance to love
and to work and to play and to look up at the stars;
to be satisfied with your possessions, but not contented
with yourself until you have made the best of them...
to think seldom of your enemies, often of your friends,
and every day of Christ; and to spend as much time as you
can, with body and with spirit in God's out-of-doors—
these are little guideposts on the footpath to peace.

HENRY VAN DYKE

God came to us because God wanted to join us
on the road, to listen to our story, and to help
us realize that we are not walking in circles
but moving toward the house of peace and joy.

HENRI J. M. NOUWEN

I wish you sunshine on your path and storms
to season your journey. I wish you peace—in the
world in which you live and in the smallest corner
of the heart where truth is kept.

ROBERT A. WARD

The LORD will give strength to His people;
the LORD will bless His people with peace.

PSALM 29:11 NKJV

Only God gives true peace—
a quiet gift He sets within us just when we
think we've exhausted our search for it.

*God's peace is joy resting.
His joy is peace dancing.*

F. F. BRUCE

# God Is for Us

Don't be afraid, I've redeemed you.
I've called your name. You're mine.
When you're in over your head, I'll be there with you.
When you're in rough waters, you will not go down.
When you're between a rock and a hard place,
it won't be a dead end—
Because I am God, your personal God,
The Holy of Israel, your Savior.
I paid a huge price for you...!
*That's* how much you mean to me!
*That's* how much I love you!

ISAIAH 43:1–4 MSG

We may...depend upon God's promises, for...He will
be as good as His word. He is so kind that He cannot
deceive us, so true that He cannot break His promise.

MATTHEW HENRY

Our days are filled with tiny golden minutes
with eternity in them. Our lives are immortal.
One thousand years from this day you will be more
alive than you are at this moment. There is a future
life with God for those who put their trust in Him.

BILLY GRAHAM

We are so preciously loved by God that
we cannot even comprehend it.
No created being can ever know
how much and how sweetly
and tenderly God loves them.

JULIAN OF NORWICH

*If God is for us, who can be against us?*

ROMANS 8:31 NKJV

# Shining Promises

However things may appear to be, of all
possible circumstances—those circumstances
in whose midst I am set—these are the best
that He could choose for me. We do not know
how this is true—where would faith be
if we did?—but we do know that all things
that happen are full of shining seed.
Light is sown for us—not darkness.

Our feelings do not affect God's facts.
They may blow up, like clouds, and cover
the eternal things that we do most truly believe.
We may not see the shining of the promises—
but they still shine! [His strength] is not for one
moment less because of our human weakness.

AMY CARMICHAEL

God has not promised skies always blue,
Flower-strewn pathways all our lives through;
God has not promised sun without rain,
Joy without sorrow, peace without pain.
But God has promised strength for the day,
Rest for the labor, light for the way,
Grace for the trials, help from above,
Unfailing sympathy, undying love.

ANNIE JOHNSON FLINT

God's promises are like the stars; the darker
the night the brighter they shine.

DAVID NICHOLAS

*But He knows the way I take;
when He has tried me,
I shall come forth as gold.*

JOB 23:10 NASB

93

# The Love of God

Who shall separate us from the love of Christ?
Shall trouble or hardship or persecution
or famine or nakedness or danger or sword?...
No, in all these things we are more than conquerors
through him who loved us. For I am convinced
that neither death nor life, neither angels nor demons,
neither the present nor the future, nor any powers,
neither height nor depth, nor anything else in all creation,
will be able to separate us from the love of God
that is in Christ Jesus our Lord.

Romans 8:35, 37–39 niv

God created the universe, but He also created you.
God knows you, God loves you, and God cares
about the tiniest details of your life.

Bruce Bickel and Stan Jantz

The grace of God means something like:
Here is your life. You might never have been,
but you *are* because the party wouldn't have been
complete without you. Here is the world. Beautiful
and terrible things will happen. Don't be afraid.
I am with you. Nothing can ever separate us.
It's for you I created the universe. I love you.

FREDERICK BUECHNER

All the things in this world are gifts and signs of God's
love to us. The whole world is a love letter from God.

PETER KREEFT

∽∼✧∼∽

*Nothing can separate you from His love,*
*absolutely nothing.... God is enough for time,*
*and God is enough for eternity. God is enough!*

HANNAH WHITALL SMITH

∽∼✧∼∽

# A Personal Invitation

God guides us, despite our uncertainties and our
vagueness, even through our failings and mistakes....
He leads us step by step, from event to event. Only
afterwards, as we look back over the way we have come
and reconsider certain important moments in our lives
in the light of all that has followed them, or when we
survey the whole progress of our lives, do we experience
the feeling of having been led without knowing it, the
feeling that God has mysteriously guided us.

PAUL TOURNIER

Listening to God is a firsthand experience.... God invites
*you* to vacation in His splendor. He invites *you* to feel the
touch of His hand. He invites *you* to feast at His table.
He wants to spend time with *you*.

MAX LUCADO

In extravagance of soul we seek His face.
In generosity of heart, we glean His gentle touch.
In excessiveness of spirit, we love Him and His
love comes back to us a hundredfold.

Tricia McCary Rhodes

God wants you to know Him as personally as He
knows you. He craves a genuine relationship with you.

Tom Richards

Grace is the central invitation to life and the final
word. It's the beckoning nudge and the overwhelming,
undeserved mercy that urges us to change and grow,
and then gives us the power to pull it off.

Tim Hansel

*Trust steadily in God, hope unswervingly, love
extravagantly. And the best of the three is love.*

1 Corinthians 13:13 msg

# My Father's World

When I look at the galaxies on a clear night—
when I look at the incredible brilliance of creation,
and think that this is what God is like, then
instead of feeling intimidated and diminished by it,
I am enlarged—I rejoice that I am part of it.

MADELEINE L'ENGLE

Above all give me grace to use these beauties
of earth without me and this eager stirring
of life within me as a means whereby my
soul may rise from creature to Creator,
and from nature to nature's God.

JOHN BAILLIE

This is my Father's world;
He shines in all that's fair.
In the rustling grass I hear Him pass;
He speaks to me everywhere.

MALTBIE D. BABCOCK

Why did God give us imaginations?
Because they help unfold His kingdom. Imagination
unveils the Great Imaginer. In the beginning,
God created. He imagined the world into being.
Every flower, animal, mountain, and rainbow
is a product of God's creative imagination.

JILL M. RICHARDSON

How beautiful it is to be alive!
To wake each morn as if the Maker's grace
Did us afresh from nothingness derive,
That we might sing "...How beautiful it is to be alive."

HENRY SEPTIMUS SUTTON

*In the beginning God created the heavens
and the earth.... God saw all that he had made,
and it was very good.*

GENESIS 1:1, 31 NIV

# Ever Present

When I walk by the wayside, He is along
with me.... Amid all my forgetfulness
of Him, He never forgets me.

THOMAS CHALMERS

God walks with us.... He scoops us up in His
arms or simply sits with us in silent strength
until we cannot avoid the awesome recognition
that yes, even now, He is here.

GLORIA GAITHER

There's not a tint that paints the rose
Or decks the lily fair,
Or marks the humblest flower that grows,
But God has placed it there....
There's not a place on earth's vast round,
In ocean's deep or air,
Where love and beauty are not found,
For God is everywhere.

No matter what our past may have held,
and no matter how many future days we have,
[God] stands beside us and loves us.

GARY SMALLEY AND JOHN TRENT

At every moment, God is calling your name and
waiting to be found. To each cry of "O Lord,"
God answers, "I am here."

God is the sunshine that warms us, the rain
that melts the frost and waters the young plants.
The presence of God is a climate of strong and
bracing love, always there.

JOAN ARNOLD

*God is our refuge and strength,
an ever-present help in trouble.
Therefore we will not fear.*

PSALM 46:1–2 NIV

# Calm Me, Lord

I will let God's peace infuse every part of today.
As the chaos swirls and life's demands pull
at me on all sides, I will breathe in God's peace
that surpasses all understanding. He has promised
that He would set within me a peace too
deeply planted to be affected by
unexpected or exhausting demands.

WENDY MOORE

Calm me, O Lord, as You stilled the storm,
Still me, O Lord, keep me from harm.
Let all the tumult within me cease,
Enfold me, Lord, in Your peace.

CELTIC TRADITIONAL

Let your faith in Christ, the omnipresent One,
be in the quiet confidence that He will every day
and every moment keep you as the apple of His eye,
keep you in perfect peace.

ANDREW MURRAY

Don't fret or worry. Instead of worrying, pray.
Let petitions and praises shape your worries into
prayers, letting God know your concerns. Before
you know it, a sense of God's wholeness, everything
coming together for good, will come and settle you
down. It's wonderful what happens when Christ
displaces worry at the center of your life.

PHILIPPIANS 4:6–7 MSG

God cannot give us a happiness and peace
apart from Himself, because it is not there.
There is no such thing.

*Nothing in all creation is so like God as stillness.*

MEISTER ECKHART

# Treasure in Nature

If we are children of God, we have a tremendous
treasure in nature and will realize that it is holy
and sacred. We will see God reaching out to us in
every wind that blows, every sunrise and sunset,
every cloud in the sky, every flower that blooms,
and every leaf that fades.

OSWALD CHAMBERS

Jesus Christ opens wide the doors of the treasure
house of God's promises, and bids us go in and
take with boldness the riches that are ours.

CORRIE TEN BOOM

The longer I live, the more my mind dwells upon
the beauty and the wonder of the world.

JOHN BURROUGHS

Go outside, to the fields, enjoy nature and the
sunshine, go out and try to recapture happiness
in yourself and in God. Think of all the beauty
that's still left in and around you and be happy!

ANNE FRANK

The miracles of nature do not seem miracles
because they are so common. If no one had ever
seen a flower, even a dandelion would be the
most startling event in the world.

Among our treasures are such wonderful things
as the grace of Christ, the love of Christ,
the joy and peace of Christ.

L. B. COWMAN

*The heavens declare the glory of God;
And the firmament shows His handiwork.*

PSALM 19:1 NKJV

# My Help

I will lift up my eyes to the hills—
from whence comes my help?
My help comes from the LORD,
who made heaven and earth.
He will not allow your foot to be moved;
He who keeps you will not slumber.
Behold, He who keeps Israel
shall neither slumber nor sleep.
The LORD is your keeper;
the LORD is your shade at your right hand.
The sun shall not strike you by day,
nor the moon by night.
The LORD shall preserve you from all evil;
He shall preserve your soul.
The LORD shall preserve
your going out and your coming in
from this time forth, and even forevermore.

PSALM 121:1–8 NKJV

No matter how long we are on this earth, the more we have to realize that life finds us living every day with the unanswered and the unresolved. Faith helps us to live with the unanswered. Hope helps us to live with the unresolved. Trust helps us to accept...and go on with the work of living.

MARK CONNOLLY

When faced with a mountain, I will not quit! I will keep on striving until I climb over, find a pass through, tunnel underneath, or simply stay and turn the mountain into a gold mine with God's help.

DR. ROBERT SCHULLER

*We have a Father in heaven who is almighty, who loves His children...and whose very joy and delight it is to...help them at all times.*

GEORGE MUELLER

# The Beauty of God's Peace

In comparison with this big world, the human heart
is only a small thing. Though the world is so large, it
is utterly unable to satisfy this tiny heart. Our ever
growing soul and its capacities can be satisfied only in
the infinite God. As water is restless until it reaches its
level, so the soul has no peace until it rests in God.

SADHU SUNDAR SINGH

God's holy beauty comes near you, like a spiritual scent,
and it stirs your drowsing soul.... He creates in you
the desire to find Him and run after Him—to follow
wherever He leads you, and to press peacefully against
His heart wherever He is.

JOHN OF THE CROSS

Peace is a margin of power around our daily need.
Peace is a consciousness of springs too deep
for earthly droughts to dry up.

HARRY EMERSON FOSDICK

Drop Thy still dews of quietness
till all our strivings cease;
take from our souls the strain and stress,
and let our ordered lives confess
the beauty of Thy peace.

JOHN GREENLEAF WHITTIER

If peace be in the heart the wildest winter storm
is full of solemn beauty.

C. F. RICHARDSON

*Be still, and know that I am God.*

PSALM 46:10 NKJV

# Praise Him!

Does not all nature around me praise God? If I were silent, I should be an exception to the universe. Does not the thunder praise Him as it rolls like drums in the march of the God of armies? Do not the mountains praise Him when the woods upon their summits wave in adoration? Does not the lightning write His name in letters of fire? Has not the whole earth a voice? And shall I, can I, silent be?

CHARLES H. SPURGEON

O God, great and wonderful, who has created the heavens, dwelling in the light and beauty of it...teach me to praise You, even as the lark which offers her song at daybreak.

ISIDORE OF SEVILLE

Let's praise His name! He is holy, He is almighty. He is love. He brings hope, forgiveness, heart cleansing, peace, and power. He is our deliverer and coming King. Praise His wonderful name!

LUCILLE M. LAW

Then your light will break forth like the dawn, and your healing will quickly appear; then your righteousness will go before you, and the glory of the LORD will be your rear guard.

ISAIAH 58:8 NIV

*When morning gilds the skies,*
*My heart awakening cries:*
*May Jesus Christ be praised!*

JOSEPH BARNBY

# God of Compassion

Tuck [this] thought into your heart today.
Treasure it. Your Father God cares about
your daily everythings that concern you.

KAY ARTHUR

The LORD!
The God of compassion and mercy!
I am slow to anger
and filled with unfailing love and faithfulness.
I lavish unfailing love to a thousand generations.

EXODUS 34:6–7 NLT

Strength, rest, guidance, grace, help, sympathy,
love—all from God to us! What a list of blessings!

EVELYN STENBOCK

God is as near as a whispered prayer
No matter the time or place,
Whether skies are blue
And all's right with you,
Or clouds dim the road you face.
In His mercy and great compassion
He will ease, He will help, He will share!
Whatever your lot,
Take heart in the thought:
God's as near as a whispered prayer!

JOHN GILBERT

God in His ample love embraces our love
with...a sort of tenderness, and we must
tread the way to Him hand in hand.

SHELDON VANAUKEN

*The loving God we serve has
immeasurable compassion and tenderness
toward each of us throughout our lives.*

DR. JAMES DOBSON

# Faithful Guide

God, who has led you safely on so far, will lead you
on to the end. Be altogether at rest in the loving
holy confidence which you ought to have in His
heavenly Providence.

FRANCIS DE SALES

Guidance is a sovereign act. Not merely does God
will to guide us by showing us His way...whatever
mistakes we may make, we shall come safely home.
Slippings and strayings there will be, no doubt, but
the everlasting arms are beneath us; we shall be
caught, rescued, restored. This is God's promise;
this is how good He is. And our self-distrust, while
keeping us humble, must not cloud the joy with
which we lean on our faithful covenant God.

J. I. PACKER

Trust the past to the mercy of God, the present
to His love, and the future to His Providence.

AUGUSTINE

A new path lies before us;
We're not sure where it leads;
But God goes on before us,
Providing all our needs.
This path, so new, so different
Exciting as we climb,
Will guide us in His perfect will
Until the end of time.

LINDA MAURICE

*When we obey him, every path
he guides us on is fragrant
with his loving-kindness and his truth.*

PSALM 25:10 TLB

# A God of Grace

Look deep within yourself and recognize what brings life and grace into your heart. It is this that can be shared with those around you. You are loved by God. This is an inspiration to love.

CHRISTOPHER DE VINCK

The Lord's chief desire is to reveal Himself to you and, in order for Him to do that, He gives you abundant grace. The Lord gives you the experience of enjoying His presence. He touches you, and His touch is so delightful that, more than ever, you are drawn inwardly to Him.

MADAME JEANNE GUYON

The ultimate test of our spirituality is the measure of our amazement at the grace of God.

D. MARTYN LLOYD-JONES

To be grateful is to recognize the Love of God in everything He has given us—and He has given us everything. Every breath we draw is a gift of His love, every moment of existence is a gift of grace, for it brings with it immense graces from Him.

THOMAS MERTON

Grace comes into the soul, as the morning sun into the world; first a dawning, then a light; and at last the sun in his full and excellent brightness.

THOMAS ADAMS

*Set your hope fully on the grace to be given you when Jesus Christ is revealed.*

1 PETER 1:13 NIV

# In His Care

God cares for the world He created, from the rising
of a nation to the falling of the sparrow. Everything
in the world lies under the watchful gaze of His
providential eyes, from the numbering of the days of
our life to the numbering of the hairs on our head.

KEN GIRE

Tonight I will sleep beneath Your feet,
O Lord of the mountains and valleys,
ruler of the trees and vines. I will rest in Your love,
with You protecting me as a father protects his children,
with You watching over me as a mother watches
over her children. Then tomorrow the sun will rise
and I will not know where I am; but I know
that You will guide my footsteps.

What is the price of two sparrows—one copper coin?
But not a single sparrow can fall to the ground
without your Father knowing it. And the very hairs
on your head are all numbered.

MATTHEW 10:29–30 NLT

When we allow God the privilege of shaping our lives,
we discover new depths of purpose and meaning. What
a joyful thought to realize you are a chosen vessel for
God—perfectly suited for His use.

JONI EARECKSON TADA

You are God's created beauty and the focus
of His affection and delight.

JANET L. SMITH

*We have been in God's thought from all eternity,*
*and in His creative love, His attention never leaves us.*

MICHAEL QUOIST

# What God Wants

God longs to give favor—that is, spiritual strength
and health—to those who seek Him, and Him
alone. He grants spiritual favors and victories,
not because the one who seeks Him is holier than
anyone else, but in order to make His holy beauty
and His great redeeming power known.... For it
is through the living witness of others that we are
drawn to God at all. It is because of His creatures,
and His work in them, that we come to praise Him.

TERESA OF AVILA

God doesn't care so much about being analyzed.
Mainly—like any parent, like any lover—
God wants to be loved.

PHILIP YANCEY

It is God's will that we believe that we see Him continually, though it seems to us that the sight be only partial; and through this belief He makes us always to gain more grace, for God wishes to be seen, and He wishes to be sought, and He wishes to be expected, and He wishes to be trusted.

JULIAN OF NORWICH

Seek the LORD your God, and you will find Him if you seek Him with all your heart and with all your soul.

DEUTERONOMY 4:29 NKJV

*To seek God means first of all to let yourself be found by Him.*

# Delight in the Lord

Delight yourself in the LORD
and he will give you the desires of your heart.
Commit your way to the LORD;
trust in him and he will do this:
He will make your righteousness shine like the dawn,
the justice of your cause like the noonday sun.

PSALM 37:4–6 NIV

God's pursuit of praise from us and our pursuit of
pleasure in Him are one and the same pursuit.
God's quest to be glorified and our quest to be satisfied
reach their goal in this one experience: our delight in
God which overflows in praise.

JOHN PIPER

Just slipping quietly into the presence of God can be so exotic and fresh that it delights us enormously.

RICHARD J. FOSTER

Dear Lord, grant me the grace of wonder.
Surprise me, amaze me, awe me in every crevice
of Your universe. Delight me to see how Your
Christ plays in ten thousand places...to the
Father through the features of men's faces.
Each day enrapture me with Your marvelous
things without number. I do not ask to see
the reason for it all; I ask only to share
the wonder of it all.

ABRAHAM JOSHUA HESCHEL

*Our fulfillment comes in knowing God's glory,
loving Him for it, and delighting in it.*

# His Inward Voice

Retire from the world each day to some private spot.... Stay in the secret place till the surrounding noises begin to fade out of your heart and a sense of God's presence envelops you.... Listen for the inward Voice till you learn to recognize it.... Give yourself to God and then be what and who you are without regard to what others think.... Learn to pray inwardly every moment.

A.W. Tozer

Enter into the inner chamber of your mind. Shut out all things save God and whatever may aid you in seeking God; and having barred the door of your chamber, seek Him.

Anselm of Canterbury

Within each of us there is an inner place
where the living God Himself longs to dwell,
our sacred center of belief.

He who has faith has...an inward reservoir of
courage, hope, confidence, calmness, and assuring
trust that all will come out well—even though to
the world it may appear to come out most badly.

B. C. FORBES

I will remember that when I give Him my heart,
God chooses to live within me—body and soul.
And I know He really is as close as breathing,
His very Spirit inside of me.

*I pray that out of his glorious riches
he may strengthen you with power
through his Spirit in your inner being.*

EPHESIANS 3:16 NIV

# A Dependable Stronghold

The LORD is my light and my salvation—
whom shall I fear?
The LORD is the stronghold of my life—
of whom shall I be afraid?...
One thing I ask of the LORD,
this is what I seek:
that I may dwell in the house of the LORD
all the days of my life,
to gaze upon the beauty of the LORD
and to seek him in his temple.
For in the day of trouble
he will keep me safe in his dwelling;
he will hide me in the shelter of his tabernacle
and set me high upon a rock....
Hear my voice when I call, O LORD;
be merciful to me and answer me.
My heart says of you, "Seek his face!"
Your face, LORD, I will seek.

PSALM 27:1, 4–5, 7–8 NIV

[God] is looking for people who will come in simple dependence upon His grace, and rest in simple faith upon His greatness. At this very moment, He's looking at you.

JACK HAYFORD

Because we are spiritual beings...it is for our good, individually and collectively, to live our lives in interactive dependence upon God.

DALLAS WILLARD

Leave behind your fear and dwell on the lovingkindness of God, that you may recover by gazing on Him.

*The more we depend on God the more dependable we find He is.*

SIR CLIFF RICHARD

# Come to the Water

Come, all you who are thirsty,
come to the waters;
and you who have no money,
come, buy and eat!
Come, buy wine and milk
without money and without cost.

Why spend money on what is not bread,
and your labor on what does not satisfy?
Listen, listen to me, and eat what is good,
and your soul will delight in the richest of fare.

Give ear and come to me;
hear me, that your soul may live.
I will make an everlasting covenant with you.

ISAIAH 55:1–3 NIV

Jesus...has been waiting all along for us
to bring our needy selves to Him and receive
from Him that eternal water.

DORIS GAILEY

We must drink deeply from the very Source the deep
calm and peace of interior quietude and refreshment
of God, allowing the pure water of divine grace to flow
plentifully and unceasingly from the Source itself.

MOTHER TERESA

Is anyone thirsty? Come!
All who will, come and drink,
Drink freely of the Water of Life!

REVELATION 22:17 MSG

*God bless you and utterly satisfy
your heart...with Himself.*

AMY CARMICHAEL

# For Himself

We desire many things, and God offers us only one thing. He can offer us only one thing—Himself. He has nothing else to give. There is nothing else to give.

PETER KREEFT

The first time God gave Himself a name
in the Bible, He called Himself the "I AM."
He is the one who is from eternity to eternity.
He is the one who never changes.

JOANIE GARBORG

Although it be good to think upon the kindness of God, and to love Him and worship Him for it; yet it is far better to gaze upon the pure essence of Him and to love Him and worship Him for Himself.

There is an essential connection between
experiencing God, loving God, and trusting God.
You will trust God only as much as you love Him,
and you will love Him to the extent you have
touched Him, rather that He has touched you.

BRENNAN MANNING

The reason for loving God is God Himself,
and the measure in which we should love Him
is to love Him without measure.

BERNARD OF CLAIRVAUX

You alone are the LORD. You made the heavens...
the earth and all that is on it, the seas and all that
is in them. You give life to everything, and the
multitudes of heaven worship you.

NEHEMIAH 9:6 NIV

*Joy is perfect acquiescence in God's will because
the soul delights itself in God Himself.*

H. W. WEBB-PEPLOE

# Totally Aware

God is every moment totally aware of each one of us.
Totally aware in intense concentration and love....
No one passes through any area of life, happy or tragic,
without the attention of God.

EUGENIA PRICE

Because God is responsible for our welfare, we are told
to cast all our care upon Him, for He cares for us. God
says, "I'll take the burden—don't give it a thought—
leave it to Me." God is keenly aware that
we are dependent upon Him for life's necessities.

BILLY GRAHAM

God reads the secrets of the heart.
God reads its most intimate feelings,
even those which we are not aware of.

JEAN-NICHOLAS GROU

If you believe in God, it is not too difficult to believe that
He is concerned about the universe and all the events
on this earth. But the really staggering message of the
Bible is that this same God cares deeply about you and
your identity and the events of your life.

BRUCE LARSON

We sometimes fear to bring our troubles to God,
because they must seem so small to Him who sits
on the circle of the earth. But if they are
large enough to vex and endanger our welfare,
they are large enough to touch His heart of love.

R. A. TORREY

God's designs regarding you, and His methods of
bringing about these designs, are infinitely wise.

MADAME JEANNE GUYON

*Live carefree before God;
he is most careful with you.*

1 PETER 5:7 MSG

# God's Nearness

Do you believe that God is near? He wants you to.
He wants you to know that He is in the midst of
your world. Wherever you are as you read these
words, He is present. In your car. On the plane.
In your office, your bedroom, your den. He's near.
And He is more than near. He is active.

MAX LUCADO

I have sought Thy nearness;
With all my heart have I called Thee,
And going out to meet Thee
I found Thee coming toward me.

YEHUDA HALEVI

Have confidence in God's mercy, for when you think
He is a long way from you, He is often quite near.

THOMAS À KEMPIS

God still draws near to us in the ordinary,
commonplace, everyday experiences and places....
He comes in surprising ways.

HENRY GARIEPY

Jesus said that He tells His friends all that
His Father has told Him; close friends communicate
thoroughly and make a transfer of heart
and thought. How awesome is our opportunity
to be friends with God, the almighty Creator of all!

BEVERLY LaHAYE

It is God to whom and with whom we travel,
and while He is the End of our journey,
He is also at every stopping place.

ELISABETH ELLIOT

God knows the rhythm of my spirit and knows
my heart thoughts. He is as close as breathing.

*Draw near to God and He will draw near to you.*

JAMES 4:8 NASB

# He Keeps His Word

For as the rain comes down, and the snow from heaven, and do not return there, but water the earth, and make it bring forth and bud, that it may give seed to the sower and bread to the eater, so shall My word be that goes forth from My mouth; it shall not return to Me void, but it shall accomplish what I please, and it shall prosper in the thing for which I sent it.

Isaiah 55:10–11 nkjv

God writes with a pen that never blots,
speaks with a tongue that never slips,
and acts with a hand that never fails.

Hubert van Zeller

Be assured, if you walk with Him and look to Him and expect help from Him, He will never fail you.

GEORGE MUELLER

God speaks to the crowd, but His call comes to individuals, and through their personal obedience He acts. He does not promise them nothing but success, or even final victory in this life.... God does not promise that He will protect them from trials, from material cares, from sickness, from physical or moral suffering. He promises only that He will be with them in all these trials, and that He will sustain them if they remain faithful to Him.

PAUL TOURNIER

*God is the God of promise. He keeps His word, even when that seems impossible.*

COLIN URQUHART

*Faith is a reasoning trust,
a trust which reckons thoughtfully and
confidently upon the trustworthiness of God.*

JOHN R. STOTT